THE SWIFT PARAKEET
Cyril Laubscher

THE PARROT SOCIETY UK
SPECIAL EDITION

© This edition published in 1999 by
Cyril Laubscher
44 Mosyer Drive, Orpington, Kent BR5 4PW, England

Contents

This edition published in 1999 by
© Cyril Laubscher
Printed and bound in England
ISBN 0-9500306-5-1

Produced by Cyril Laubscher
Designed by Joy Mutter, Picture Graphics
Illustrator Graham Parrish
Photographers Cyril Laubscher, Chris Tzaros,
Bev Sharman, Kerry Febey, Colin Lawrence

Reproduction Bantam Litho Ltd, Essex, UK
Printed by Principal Colour Ltd, UK

INTRODUCTION

n July 1998, Keith Satterthwaite and David Coombes from The Parrot Society approached me about producing a special publication that could be distributed to members to mark the start of the new millennium. Keith suggested that we should consider the Swift Parakeet and I agreed to the idea immediately, as it is one of the most interesting parrots.

Why publish a book on the Swift Parakeet" as it is only one of some 340+ parrot species around the world. However, by the end of this book, the reader will fully understand why this parakeet was chosen.

With the knowledge that I had gained over the years, I knew that the Swift Parakeet would provide enough interesting material as it was then listed as vulnerable under the Federal Endangered Species Protection Act 1992, and by the Tasmanian authorities under the Tasmanian Threatened Species Protection Act 1995. In 1999, the status of the Swift Parakeet was revised using the current IUCN criteria, and is now listed as endangered nationally.

The puzzling question as to why European breeders are successful in raising young while Australian breeders seem to have difficulties needed investigating, along with the scientific aspect of why this species is now endangered in the wild.

The Swift Parrot is an enigma" was the opening sentence written in the introduction to *THE SWIFT PARROT – A Report on its ecology, distribution and status, including management consideration*, which was prepared by Peter Brown of the Department of Lands Parks and Wildlife, Tasmania, for the Australian Heritage Commission in July 1989. The ground-breaking report highlighted the plight of the Swift Parrot in the wild, and prompted an ongoing scientific research study into its status.

While planning the research for this book, it soon became apparent that a trip to Tasmania during the breeding season of the Swift Parakeet was necessary.

There, I met with Peter Brown, Raymond Brereton, and Mark Holdsworth of the Nature Conservation Branch of the Department of Primary Industry, Water and Environment in Hobart. After spending some time with them in the field – photographically recording the Swift Parakeet in its natural environment during the breeding season – I realised that there is a wealth of information already available through the efforts of the Swift Parrot Recovery Team.

To complement the scientific research, an avicultural research programme was undertaken to obtain details from breeders of Swift Parakeets among the members of various societies including The Parrot Society (UK); Parkieten Sociëteit (Holland); and Club des Oiseaux Exotique (France). Similar research was conducted in other countries including Australia, Belgium, Canada, Denmark, Germany, Greenland, Switzerland, and the USA. A total of 72 questionnaires with information on housing, feeding, and breeding Swift Parakeets were returned. While this is only a small number of the breeders around the world, it certainly illustrates how much interest there is in this colourful parakeet.

All the information received has added greatly to the knowledge available. So much so, that the original concept of doing a booklet on the avicultural status and what is happening in breeders aviaries, has expanded into a much more meaningful and enlightening study. This book is the culmination of a great deal of effort provided by many people around the world who have willingly contributed, and, who are deeply concerned about the survival of this beautiful parakeet in the wild and in aviculture.

The Swift Parakeet is a Tasmanian breeding endemic that overwinters on the mainland. At present, it is the subject of a scientific ecological study to establish why the population is in decline. Protecting its feeding habitat is one of the important aspects of the Swift Parrot Recovery Plan.

Sexing these attractive parakeets can present some difficulty, but it is immediately apparent that there is a sexual difference in this young pair. The brighter coloured male is on the left. © *Cyril Laubscher*

THE SWIFT PARAKEET

amed after the British ornithologist Dr. John Latham, the genus *Lathamus* comprises only one species The Swift Parakeet *L. discolor*. This nectar-feeding parrot inhabits Tasmania during the breeding season in pring and summer, and migrates to the Australian mainland in winter, as do two other Tasmanian arakeets – the Blue-winged Parakeet *Neophema chrysostoma*, and the endangered Orange-bellied arakeet *N. chrysogaster*.

Australia, the unique Swift Parakeet is generally known as the Swift Parrot in ornithological literature nd circles. It is also referred to as Swift Lorikeet, Swift-flying Parakeet or Lorikeet, Red-faced Parrot or arakeet, and, Red-shouldered Parrot or Parakeet (Forshaw 1981).

n arboreal species that is seldom seen on the ground, except when bathing in a small pool or puddle of rater, a Swift Parakeet may occasionally fly down to pick up a blossom, or fruit, that it had dropped while reding on it. Small flocks can often be seen in the suburbs of Hobart and other towns in the south- astern and northern coastal areas, where they feed on eucalyptus blossom, and breed in suitable calities. Swift Parakeets are regular visitors to the local golf course at Burnie in northern Tasmania.

hey start to migrate across the Bass Strait to the Australian mainland during late February and March, and y April virtually the whole population has completed the migration. A few stay behind, mostly in the orth of Tasmania, although there has been an occasional sighting of small groups in winter in a number f places, including Hobart, Swansea, and in Spreyton.

wift Parakeets remain on the mainland until towards the end of August when they start to migrate back Tasmania. This migration continues through till October. Throughout the winter, they move around in omadic manner, foraging for nectar and lerp. The available food sources dictate their movements, which

in vary from year to ar. The main areas here Swift Parakeets e seen in winter xtend from south- astern South Australia rough Victoria to New uth Wales, then onto uthern Queensland. he major oncentrations are ound central Victoria.

he remarkable Swift arakeet has been an nigma for taxonomists nce it was first iscovered. Only recently as it become the bject of close scrutiny, d it is now, regrettably, sted as endangered ationally. The following ages will outline some f the scientific, and icultural, work that is eing done to try and ve this delightful arakeet, for future enerations.

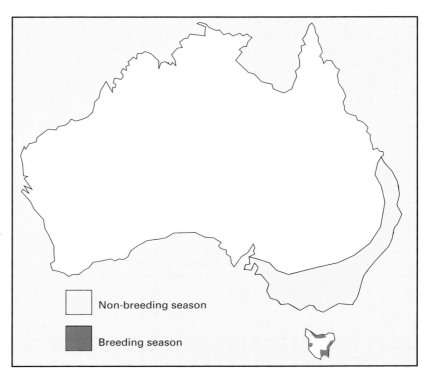

Non-breeding season

Breeding season

Distribution of the swift parrot in Australia.

DESCRIPTION

The numerous photographs in this book illustrate the most important features of male and female. However, for a detailed description, I have followed Forshaw's *Australian Parrots* (1981).

Length 25 cm (10 inches). Females can vary between 23-25 cm (9-10 inches).
ADULT MALE: General plumage bright green, lighter and more yellowish on the underparts; forehead, throat and foreparts of cheeks red; lores and borders of red facial areas yellow; turquoise-blue suffusion on ear-coverts; crown dark blue; some birds have few red feathers on underparts; vent and under tail-coverts dull red, feathers variably tipped with yellow and pale green; under wing-coverts, bend of wing and lesser wing-coverts rich red; outer median and secondary wing-coverts greenish-blue; primary-coverts and outer webs of primaries violet-blue, latter narrowly margined with pale yellow; inner webs of tertials scarlet; central tail feathers above dull brownish-red, tipped with dark blue, lateral feathers dull dark blue, margined with brownish-red; underside of tail dusky grey; underwing-stripe variable; bill brownish-horn; iris pale yellow; legs brownish.
Weight 50-74 grams

ADULT FEMALE: Similar to, but slightly duller than male; underwing-stripe variable.

IMMATURES: Noticeably duller than adults; less red on face and under tail-coverts; shorter tail; underwing-stripe present; iris brownish.

Regarding eye-colour, the iris colour appears to be a variable feature that is influenced by age and can vary from brownish-yellow or orange-yellow to yellow. Forshaw states that the iris colour of adults is yellow, and the juveniles have a brownish iris. The two eye studies featured were photographed in the research aviaries of Brett Gartrell at the University of Tasmania in Hobart.

© Cyril Laubscher

Gartrell thought that the eye colour could possibly be linked to the sex of the bird, but this has subsequently been ruled out after surgically sexing the birds.

An adult female is not normally as brightly coloured as a male, but this can be deceiving when a good female starts to resemble a poorly coloured male. When this is encountered, a female can be sexed by the underwing stripe, which is retained in adulthood in 99% of females – according to Kees Lansen (pers. comm.), from data of birds that he has bred in aviaries. The underwing-stripe is a series of oblique oval-shaped whitish marking – seen on the front cover photograph. Fledgling and immature birds feature this underwing-stripe, and are much duller than an adult. The young can take up to two years to reach full adulthood.

According to Gartrell (pers. comm.) " There is a good deal of variation occurring among individuals in the wild population. Some birds have more yellow on the underparts and red markings on the chest, especially as they reach maturity."

I have also observed this variation in avicultural populations.

A report made to Birding-aus Mailing List from David Geering, who was out with a group birding at Killawara State Forest in north-eastern Victoria during the weekend of 10-11 July 1999, came across, and saw a very vividly coloured Swift Parakeet that had a large amount of red blotched across the belly and u onto the lower breast. It was estimated that 30-40% of the underparts were red.

CLASSIFICATION

The Swift Parakeet is a monotypic species (a genus comprised of a single species) that has affinities with the broad-tailed parrots and brush-tongued lorikeets. Classifying the Swift Parakeet is a difficult problem for taxonomists to solve. In many ways – appearance, habits, and general behaviour – Swift Parrots resemble lorikeets, especially as they feed on, and forage for nectar. The brush-tipped tongue of a Swift Parakeet is similar in shape to, but not as bulky as the Obi Lory (*Eos squamata obiensis*), and is shorter than the tongue of a Stella's Lorikeet (*Charmosyna papou goliathina*). The three different tongues are illustrated for comparison purposes (note the difference in the colour of the lory's tongue).

This raises the vexing question of whether the Swift Parakeet is a lorikeet, or not. They do have similar feeding, and general habits, that are akin to a lorikeet. The evolvement of the beak and tongue to resemble that of a lorikeet is probably the result of convergent evolution (Hindwood & Sharland 1964) to aid the intake of nectar, and insects found in flowers.

The brush-tipped tongue of a Swift Parakeet is not as long as a lorikeet's. © *Cyril Laubscher*

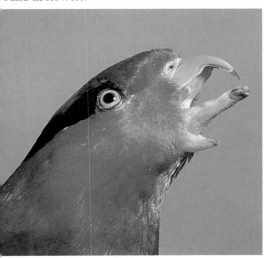

Stella's Lorikeet has possibly the longest tongue of all the lorikeets. © *Cyril Laubscher*

A Lory's tongue is shorter, broader, and stubbier. © *Cyril Laubscher*

But, as much as they resemble lorikeets in feeding habits, some scientists believe that anatomically, and taxonomically, the Swift Parakeet is more closely aligned with the broad-tailed parrot group. This is a group of Australian parrots, which include the *Psephotus* genus (Red-rumped Parakeet etc.), rosellas (*Platycercus*), Barnard's and other ringnecks in the *Barnardius* genus, blue bonnets (*Northiella*), and, the Red-capped or Pileated Parrot (*Purpureicephalus spurius*) (Christidis et al. 1991). DNA testing on the Swift Parakeet that took place in Melbourne some years ago suggested that the swift is more closely related to the rosella than a lorikeet.

Some scientists believe that anatomically, and taxonomically, the Swift Parakeet is more closely aligned with the broad-tailed parrot group. This is a group of Australian parrots, which include the *Psephotus* genus (Red-rumped Parakeet etc.), rosellas (*Platycercus*), Barnard's and other ringnecks in the *Barnardius* genus, blue bonnets (*Northiella*), and, the Red-capped or Pileated Parrot (*Purpureicephalus spurius*) (Christidis et al. 1991).

Psephotus haematonotus
Red-rumped Parakeet
© Cyril Laubscher

Purpureicephalus spurius
Pileated Parakeet
© Cyril Laubscher

Northiella haematogaster
Red-vented Blue Bonnets
Note under wing-stripe
© Cyril Laubscher

Platycercus elegans
Crimson Rosella
© Cyril Laubscher

Barnardius barnardius
Barnard's Parakeet
© Cyril Laubscher

STATUS

"The Swift Parrot is an enigma" was the opening quote in the introduction to *THE SWIFT PARROT - A Report on its ecology, distribution and status, including management consideration*, which was prepared by Peter Brown of the Department of Lands Parks and Wildlife, Tasmania, for the Australian Heritage Commission in July 1989. This ground-breaking report highlighted the plight of the Swift Parrot in the wild, and prompted an ongoing scientific research study into the status of the Swift Parrot.

Then, the Swift Parakeet was listed as vulnerable under the Federal *Endangered Species Protection Act 1992*, followed by the Tasmanian authorities listing it as vulnerable under the *Tasmanian Threatened Species Protection Act 1995*. In 1999 the status of the Swift Parakeet was revised using the current IUCN criteria and as a result it is now listed as endangered nationally.

In a recent discussion with Joseph Forshaw (well-known author of *Australian Parrots* and *Parrots of the World*), he mentioned (pers. comm.) that there is no evidence that the Swift Parrot was very numerous at any stage.

However, in recent times there has been a large amount of deforestation taking place. The destruction, and the continuing clearance of Blue Gums for agricultural and forestry purposes, has resulted in the loss of the large trees that supported the breeding population of the Swift Parakeet on the eastern coastal areas of Tasmania. The restricted breeding distribution of this parakeet is now confined to certain dry forest types that occur only within a few miles of the coast.

The resulting decline in the endemic breeding population has reduced the estimated total of breeding pairs to around 1,000 (Brereton, 1996) following the latest summer counts conducted in 1995/6.

Because much of the Blue Gum habitat is on good fertile soil in unprotected land, the authorities are greatly concerned about the survival of the Swift Parakeet. Its breeding ecology is based mainly on the flowering cycle of the Blue Gums, which is their major food source during the breeding season. Older trees produce more flowers, and consequently, more nectar. This has a direct impact on the breeding population and the decline in breeding results.

A number of other factors have to be taken into account, and will no doubt, be dealt with in due course by the various governmental authorities of each sector. The necessary cooperation has been forthcoming and positive results have already been achieved.

SWIFT PARROT RECOVERY PLAN

A national recovery plan, sponsored by the Natural Heritage Trust (a federally funded national conservation program), has been implemented involving the states of Tasmania, Victoria and New South Wales. The Swift Parrot Recovery Plan was begun in 1997 and is coordinated by Raymond Brereton, based at the Nature Conservation Branch of the Department of Primary Industry, Water and Environment in Hobart. As the Swift Parakeet Recovery Coordinator, he is responsible for the implementation of the actions in the recovery plan under the guidance of the recovery team. The Swift Parrot Recovery Team has representatives from the conservation agencies of each of the three states as well as two NGO representatives, from Birds Australia (the national birding group) and the Threatened Species Network (a World Wide Fund for Nature program).

The objectives of the recovery plan are to obtain as much information on the ecology of the Swift Parakeet nationally. This will then allow the authorities to plan, and implement, a survival programme to protect the declining population.

Swift Parakeets breed in this eucalypt woodland at Mt. Nelson. © *Cyril Laubscher*

Most importantly, the main effort is being directed at retaining the feeding habitat throughout the birds' range, and the protection of existing nesting hollows within the breeding range. Surveys have been undertaken to identify the important Swift Parakeet habitats in eastern and northern Tasmania, so that they can be protected.

Similarly, and of great significance, are the annual surveys conducted on the mainland where the Swift Parakeets over winter. The purpose of these surveys is to obtain information of numbers; locations; forest types; food resources; and which other bird species the Swift Parakeets associate with at the foraging sites. Prior to the surveys, very little was known about their movements, or, which foraging habitat was most suitable.

Two counts are conducted each year. The first survey is during a selected weekend in May, followed by the second survey during August, just before the parakeets start migrating back to Tasmania.

In 1998, more than 100 volunteer observers participated in the Swift Parrot Recovery Project winter surveys at predetermined selected sites in South Australia, Victoria, New South Wales and Queensland. The first survey in May produced 565 from 37 sites, and in August, 614 were counted from 51 sites. The total in 1998 amounted to 1164, which is a huge increase on the 1997 total of 602 birds.

Unfortunately, the figures for 1999 are not yet available for inclusion in this book.

MAINLAND WINTER SURVEYS

Victoria

Simon Kennedy is currently the Swift Parrot Project Officer on the mainland. Chris Tzaros, who has now moved on to further his studies and complete a Masters degree at Deakin University, previously held this position. A couple of Chris Tzaros photographs – taken while he was still involved in the project – are featured in this chapter.

In Victoria, Swift Parrots were found foraging mainly in Box-Ironbark forests. They were seen feeding with various lorikeets and honeyeaters. The parakeets generally chose the largest and most active of the winter flowering eucalypts. Two of the most important trees used were Grey Box (*E. microcarpa*) that flowers until May, and Red Ironbark (*E. tricarpa*). A third, the Yellow Gum (*E. leucoxylon*) that grows in open forest and woodland is also used extensively. Grey Box grows on open flats and Red Ironbark is mostly seen on ridges.

Golden Wattle (*Acacia pycnantha*) flowers in Victoria around August, and the Swift Parakeets enjoy chewing the buds, even descending to the ground to eat the ones that they have dropped.

During the winter, Swift Parakeets feed largely on nectar from various eucalypts. They also forage extensively in non-nectar producing eucalypts, for lerps, a sugary covering created by psyllid insects, which, shelter under the lerps while feeding on the leaves. This is a very important food source, especially in areas where there is not much nectar being produced. Lerps are most active in the autumn, just prior to the migration of the Swift Parrots from Tasmania.

Several areas of extensive Red Ironbark forest have been identified as prime habitat that can support large numbers of Swift Parakeets. Each season, only some of the Red Ironbarks are in flower, following a similar pattern to the Blue Gums in Tasmania. That is another reason why the parakeets may not be seen in an area for many years, and

Swift Parakeet foraging for lerp.
© Chris Tzaros

Lerp is a major food source for Swift Parakeets. © Chris Tzaros

hen suddenly, they reappear. These erratic movements make them more difficult to monitor.

An interesting account came from Tony Brindley. He saw a large group of Swift Parakeets – totalling 100's – in Walmer, near Maryborough in central Victoria in 1991. They were feeding frantically on the gum tree blossom that was flowering profusely in that area at the time. Other birds that were feeding there included Little Lorikeets (*Glossopsitta pusilla*) and Purple-crowned Lorikeets *Glossopsitta*

Red Ironbark woodland is typical wintering habitat of the Swift Parakeet at Sedgwick State Forest, central Victoria. © *Chris Tzaros*

porphyrocephala). Brindley has also observed them regularly in his garden in the Main Ridge area of Victoria.

Records show that over-wintering Swift Parakeets are most plentiful in Victoria. During the 1998 winter surveys that were conducted on the mainland, more than 85% of the Swift Parakeets counted, were from Victoria.

A small flock of Swift Parakeets drinking at a pool. © *Chris Tzaros*

Swift Parakeets in New South Wales

In New South Wales, Anthony Overs is the Threatened Species Officer with the New South Wales National Parks and Wildlife Service. Part of his responsibilities includes the Swift Parrot Project in NSW.

One of the reports that he received in May 1997 was of a sighting of around 200 Swift Parakeets that were feeding on flowering White Box (*Eucalyptus albens*) in the Capertree Valley in NSW. This is an unusual sighting to see so many birds together, and no doubt, gave the survey monitors much pleasure to record, and watch, this delightful parakeet.

In July 1999, Stan Sindel informed me that he had several sightings of Swift Parakeets in May and June after a lapse of nearly 10 years from when he last saw them feeding on Red Gum blossom in his back garden. I was hoping that I would have a chance to see them while I spent the weekend with Stan and his wife Jill, but unfortunately, the

This striking male has some red feathers on the breast, which is occasionally encountered in individuals. © *Cyril Laubscher*

parakeets were not around at the time. One of Stan's neighbours Charles Attard, had regular sightings around the outer western suburbs of Sydney in 1999.

Queensland sightings

South-eastern Queensland is generally the northernmost distribution area for Swift Parakeets, and in years gone by, it was thought that they were occasional visitors to this area. But, during four of the last five years, they were seen, and recorded regularly.

In 1998, David Rounsevell reported that between 30-50 Swift Parakeets were sighted feeding on the flowers of Forest Red Gum *E. tereticornis* between 27 July and 14 August, when the birds left the area to start the journey back to the breeding grounds in Tasmania.

The Forest Red Gum had a prolific flowering season in Queensland during 1998. Other sightings were recorded around the Toowoomba area. A report from Michael Atzeni in Toowoomba to Birding-aus Mailing List on 13 August 1998, mentioned that two Swift Parakeets had been killed in collisions with a fence around a private tennis court on the northwest outskirts of the town.

SWIFT PARAKEET REPRODUCTION STUDY

Brett Gartrell studying microscopic detail of pollen.
© Cyril Laubscher

Brett Gartrell is doing a major study into the reproduction of the Swift Parakeet for his PhD project. This involves investigating the physiological and nutritional constraints on their reproduction cycle. Various aspects of biological behaviour, including nutrition requirements, and how much influence the flowering of Blue Gums has on their breeding cycle, will be covered.

In particular, the connection between Swift Parakeet breeding success and the flowering of Blue Gum will have an important influence on future management decisions for both. A concurrent study on the pollinators of Blue Gum, by Andrew Hingston – a PhD student based at the University of Tasmania – includes observations on the feeding action of birds. The results will assist in formulating an overall biological picture.

Other answers that will be sought are: How will the reproductive ability and breeding success be affected by the continuing environmental changes? And, what are the risks of extinction?

The population decline and investigations into mortality, including disease and nutritional deficiencies will be dealt with, as they can have a significant impact on wild bird populations. Gartrell is also monitoring how the hormone levels, body condition, and the moult differ throughout the annual breeding cycle.

Anatomical Comparison Studies: With the emphasis on evolutionar

The sleek lines and good colouring of this male are immediately apparent.
© Cyril Laubscher

aspects, between Swift Parakeets, Green Rosellas and Musk Lorikeets.

Circannual Reproductive Cycle: Being studied on Swift Parakeets and Musk Lorikeets in captivity and free living.

Feeding Trials: Are being conducted in a special captive population of 17 Swift Parakeets. Pollen, and the nutritional benefits thereof, will be studied. This could have a far-reaching implication into the feeding requirements for Swift parakeets being bred around the world. Until now, very little scientific work on the use of pollen for nectar-feeding birds has been completed.

Population and Aging Studies: Using Swift Parakeets, Musk Lorikeets, and Green Rosellas.

The study will undoubtedly, greatly improve the knowledge available on the Swift Parakeet.

Green Rosella (Platycercus caledonicus) © Cyril Laubscher

Musk Lorikeet (Glossopsitta concinna) © Cyril Laubscher

RADIO TRACKING AND MONITORING

Raymond Brereton is involved with the survey into the breeding of Swift Parakeets in Tasmania. He uses various methods, including radio tracking, to monitor the movements of the elusive Swift Parakeets during the breeding season. This requires the parakeet be fitted with a special transmitter, and to accomplish this task, the parakeet has to be caught in a mist net that is positioned in known feeding areas. This usually occurs just as the breeding season is starting, or shortly thereafter.

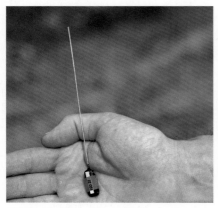

This transmitter weighs only 2 grams.
© Cyril Laubscher

Tying the transmitter to the tail feathers. © Cyril Laubscher

A tiny transmitter weighing only 2 grams is fitted to the tail feathers. The transmitter's aerial, which sticks out about 1 cm beyond the tail, sends out a regular signal, which can be picked up by the receiver on the tracking device. The unit operates up to a distance of between 1-2 km (one mile +) away. The battery power in the transmitter lasts for six weeks approximately. There is no hardship applied to the bird while carrying the transmitter, which is simply discarded when the moult starts and the tail feathers fall out.

When tied, the transmitter sticks out 1cm beyond the tail.
© Cyril Laubscher

Raymond Brereton using a tracking device to follow a Swift Parakeet on Bruny Island about 1-2 kms (1 mile) away.
© Cyril Laubscher

Raymond Brereton uses headphones to listen to signals received from a transmitter. © Cyril Laubscher

Close up of tracking device and recording apparatus. © Cyril Laubscher

Six of the 24 birds trapped at a foraging site near Woodbridge in south east Tasmania, were fitted with radio transmitters between the 22/10/98 and 4/11/98. All of the birds were banded, weighed, measured, assessed for condition and a blood sample taken for the reproductive study by Brett Gartrell.

During the ensuing six weeks, the radio tagged birds were recorded regularly and their movements monitored – a number of times per day initially, then gradually reduced to 2-3 times per week. Most of the radio tracking was done from the ground while the birds stayed near the foraging site. Then, as the birds started to disperse when the flowering period declined, a light aircraft fitted with a purpose built antennae system was used to track their movements. This supplied useful information that could not be obtained by any other means.

It was not certain whether any of the six birds that were tagged, were actively involved in breeding at the time, but three of them were constantly monitored in an area where breeding was taking place. Three Swift Parakeets were located and observed feeding on flowering Blue Gum at the capture site, while the other three were tracked to where they were feeding on other Blue Gums between 6 and 20 km away. Their movements to roosting sites were also followed, with one bird flying to its roosting site about 1 km away from the feeding site.

The tagging has provided information regarding the movements of the birds when they are foraging around the breeding areas. Most were found to stay within 5 km of the capture site up to six weeks after they were tagged. As the radio tracking progresses, the information will assist in identifying potential nesting and foraging areas, which, can then be protected by management agreement with the land owners. Voluntary assistance has already been obtained from landowners where important sites on private land have been identified.

Radio tracking within the breeding range will continue during the 1999/2000 breeding activity survey.

MASTERS OF FLIGHT FACE MID-AIR PERILS

One of the greatest attributes of the aptly named Swift Parakeet is its mastery of flight. After visiting Tasmania in December 1999 and observing them in their natural environment during the breeding season, I can only marvel at the speed with which this parakeet is able to fly. The strong direct flight as they thread their way through the trees is quite remarkable.

The breakneck speed at which they travel is also, in many instances, their downfall. The number of window-strikes and related types of accidents is causing concern.

Swift Parakeets face major perils in the form of windows and wires, as well as other man-made barriers, such as tennis court fences, and even motor vehicles. The number of deaths recorded from collisions is quite alarming. During the 1997-98 season alone, there were 39 Swift Parakeets killed in collisions in the

Hobart area. That is nearly 13% of the 500 birds recorded during that season in the area.

Fortunately, only 11 deaths from collisions occurred during the 1998-99 season, with 6 injuries recorded – 4 of which were rehabilitated. The remaining two suffered permanent wing damage, as the illustration shows.

Collisions are not surprising, when considering the speed at which Swift Parakeets can fly. Raymond Brereton and Brett Gartrell (pers. comm.) were driving back from a Swift Parakeet monitoring trip, when they recorded the following flight data. As they travelled along a straight stretch of road at a steady speed of 80 kilometres an hour (50 mph), there was a pair of Swift Parakeets flying in and out of the trees growing alongside the road, and they were maintaining the same speed as the vehicle for about 5 km (3 miles)!

After a collision, the bend of this Swift Parakeet's wing was broken off. © *Cyril Laubscher*

What is the cause of these collisions? Most deaths happen because of a rapidly flying Swift Parakeet hitting a window at high speed. Very few – if any – birds flying at the speed that a Swift is capable of attaining, could survive an impact against a solid object, such as a window, or a motor vehicle.

Tony Brindley provided a vivid account that his wife saw while visiting with friends at Kingston, south of Hobart, in 1995. She saw two Swift Parakeets fly straight through an open plate glass window under a patio, careering across the room and then slamming into another set of closed windows. Both birds died instantly!

Brett Gartrell found that of 18 birds that he examined after suffering fatal injuries, 8 of them had died from window-strikes, and two died after colliding with a motor vehicle. The birds that died from window collisions had suffered fractured wings, breastbones (keel) and shoulders. Head injuries also occurred in some deaths.

Two reports came from Queensland in 1998 of Swift Parakeets that had been killed, and injured. These were the first reports ever received of deaths resulting from collisions while over-wintering on the mainland. Both incidents involved tennis courts, which can be a major hazard for these parakeets. In one incident, two birds were

When a Swift Parakeet strikes a window or tennis court fence in full flight, it can result in a fatal injury as the breastbone is shattered. © *Cyril Laubscher*

injured at Mudgeerabah on the Gold Coast. Michael Atzeni from Toowoomba sent a message to Birding-aus Mailing List on 13 August 1998, in which he mentioned that two Swift Parakeets had been brought in to a local vet after they had been killed when they struck the side fencing of a private tennis court on the northwest outskirts of the town.

A similar situation can occur with Swift Parakeets kept in aviaries. As soon as they see a silhouette of a bird of prey, they fly into a blind panic, and there are numerous reports of them colliding with the wire fence at the end of their aviaries, sometimes with fatal results.

This sort of hazard should be fairly easy to overcome, simply by planting some sort of foliage, or creeper on a frame situated in front of the wire fence in an aviary, or at a tennis court. Alternatively, there should be some sort of artificial screening available, such as shade cloth that would accomplish the desired effect, without incurring a heavy financial outlay. Large, fast growing trees could also provide a screen within a short while.

Efforts are under way to improve the visibility of hazards – such as tennis courts and windows – identified by the collision hot spot program. Improving the visibility of a tennis court is definitely easier than a window, which could undoubtedly be affected by loss of light, depending on what type of screening is undertaken. Window boxes can provide some protection.

Urban developments are now being targeted to increase awareness among developers of the hazards facing Swift Parakeets and mid-air collisions. Planning guidelines for mitigating bird strikes are being submitted for inclusion in planning schemes being developed by local governments in Tasmania.

A collisions pamphlet is being published to highlight the problem of identified collision hot spots. This will be distributed to local government authorities, householders and schools.

FEEDING AND BREEDING IN TASMANIA

The main breeding areas for Swift Parakeets are concentrated on the eastern side of Tasmania, including the capital city of Hobart. They can be seen in many of the suburban areas, especially where Blue Gum (*Eucalyptus globulus*) is flowering. Swifts rely heavily on the nectar of Blue Gum, and will normally only be seen breeding where they are in bloom.

The breeding area in Tasmania is shown on the accompanying map. The main area is a solid colour, and the secondary, or northern breeding area, is the lighter shaded portion.

Raymond Brereton took me to see one of the 1997 nesting hollows (illustrated) at Mt. Nelson, just south of Hobart. He told me that the nesting hollow is seldom used in consecutive years, which raised the question "why not"? The answer was simple enough – the Swift Parakeet breeds in areas where Blue Gums are generally in flower, and as the trees often only flower profusely, with abundant nectar flow, every second season, the parakeets usually have to use a different breeding tree each season.

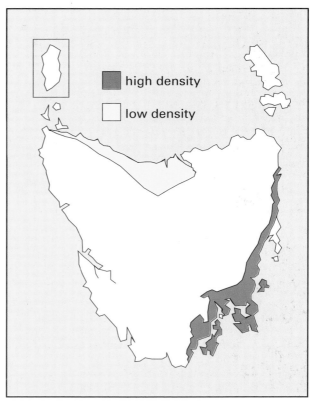

high density

low density

Breeding distribution of the Swift Parakeet.

Raymond Brereton standing at the base of a large Blue Gum tree in which Swift Parakeets nested previously. INSET: Nest-hole about 20m (65 feet) high in this Blue Gum. © *Cyril Laubscher*

They often breed, and feed, in loose colonies or groups, similar to lorikeets. Obviously, this makes monitoring their movements more difficult. If they used the same nest every year, that would make it easier to inspect during a given period each year.

The nest was positioned fairly high in the tree, somewhere around 20 metres up. In the picture, Raymond Brereton is standing at the bottom of the tree, looking dwarfed by the size of the surrounding trees. Even when breeding, Swift Parakeets are gregarious, and sometimes, two nests can be found in the same tree. The female prepares the nest site, and eggs are normally laid early in October, but can be laid up to the beginning of December. The average clutch size is 4-5 eggs, and incubation lasts for 19-20 days.

Although the breeding of Swift Parakeets coincides with the flowering season of the Blue Gum, they do also take nectar from the Black or Swamp Gum (*Eucalyptus ovata*) – the Blue Gum providing nearly 80% and the Black Gum just over 10% of the nectar consumed in Tasmania (Brown 1989).

A close up of Blue Gum flowers to show the gumnut in which, hundreds of special sacs known as nectaries, produce the nectar. © *Cyril Laubscher*

The amount of nectar in each white blossom of a Blue Gum that is producing nectar is quite remarkable. I managed to pick a small cluster of about three flowers from the tree in the photograph. The blossoms were kept overnight in a plastic bag, so that I could do close up photographs of the flowers the following morning. Much to my surprise, the bag contained about two tablespoonfuls of nectar.

The white Blue Gum flower is the largest of all the Tasmanian

This flowering Blue Gum was in full nectar flow during the middle of the breeding season on Bruny Island, south of Hobart. © *Cyril Laubscher*

eucalypts, and develops inside a thick, ribbed woody capsule, better known as a gumnut. Inside the gumnut, hundreds of special sacs known as nectaries, produce the nectar. The nectaries fill up daily, releasing the nectar into the gumnut for birds, animals and insects to feast on. Brown (1989) mentioned that in one test, a Blue Gum flowering in July was producing nectar at the rate of .15 ml in each flower over a 24 hour period, whereas, in *E. ficifolia* only .005 ml was recorded – the Blue Gum nectar production was 30 times greater!

Blue Gum trees growing in close proximity, can have different flowering times, with varying amounts of nectar flow between trees. One that I found flowering at the University of Tasmania in July 1999, did not produce any nectar in the flowers that I tested by placing them in a bag overnight, in a similar way to the overnight method described above. However, there could be a different result between September and December when the tree was in full bloom.

Lerp is another food source that is avidly consumed. Lerp is a sugary covering excreted by small psyllid insects, which, shelter under the lerps while attacking and feeding on the eucalyptus leaves. Forshaw in *Australian Parrots 1981* mentions two types of lerp that are consumed. *Glycaspis* lerps protect themselves by excreting a sugary substance, and also excrete large amounts of a sweet liquid. *Lasiopsylla* lerps shelter under a whitish covering. The parakeets eat the lerps, covering, and the insects.

However, Swift Parrots do not eat as much lerp in Tasmania as they do when overwintering on the mainland. Brereton has estimated lerp consumption in Tasmania at 5% of their diet. Other food consumed, includes fruit, berries, native grass seeds and other vegetable matter. Insects, including caterpillars, form part of their diet. Sand and grit are also consumed, possibly to aid digestion.

When feeding on nectar, Swift Parakeets virtually bury their beaks in the blossom to make sure that they capture as much of the nectar available from each flower. These acrobatic parakeets often hang upside down while feeding on the rich nectar source from eucalypts. There are reports of them hanging upside down, with nectar dribbling from the side of the beak after feasting.

They are readily seen in the centre of Hobart, and Mark Holdsworth pointed out a site that is frequently used by Swift Parakeets – a car park in front of a large hardware shopping complex, where these parakeets congregate to feed on the plentiful supply of nectar in the eucalyptus blossom.

A Swift Parakeet virtually buries its beak in the blossom to capture as much of the nectar from each flower. © Cyril Laubscher

After patiently waiting, some interesting pictures of the Swift Parakeets feeding in the trees were obtained. It was difficult

This car park in front of a hardware store in Hobart, has Swift Parakeets flying in to feed on the nectar and pollen in the flowering eucalypts during the breeding season. © Cyril Laubscher

A Swift Parakeet is constantly on the move when feeding on blossoms in a tree. © Cyril Laubscher

to get a clear view of the birds as they crept through the branches to get to the next flower, but the end result was worth it. They often hang upside down while sipping nectar, or nibble at lerps under the leaves.

Their soft, tuneful notes are the easiest way to locate the birds while they feed in the trees. Much bickering takes place and the noise can escalate, especially as they chase each other away from the tree where they are feeding. As they fly away, their metallic-like disyllabic *clink-clink* or *kik-kik-kik* contact and alarm call is heard. It is often repeated in quick succession – between 20-30 times in 10 seconds (Brown 1989) – as they fly around from tree to tree in a feeding patch. The calls of a Swift Parakeet all have a melodious, piping tone that is pleasant on the ear, unlike the abrasive screeching notes of lorikeets.

As the Blue Gum nectar flow diminishes, other eucalypts provide the nectar that is required. The majority of the population disperses from their breeding grounds as they prepare for their migratory crossing of the Bass Strait to the mainland. Because of the speed at which they can fly (70-80 kilometres – 45-50 miles per hour), Swift Parakeets probably have no great difficulty in completing the 300 kilometre (187 miles) crossing in one day.

Gartrell states (in litt.) "My overall impression is that the Swift Parakeet is primarily a nectarivorous and insectivorous bird. The enlarged gizzard allows it to use seed in captivity, but this is not its "natural" diet. While nectar plays an important role in energy supply especially during the breeding season, pollen and insects are needed to fulfil its protein requirements"

They gradually move up the western side where food sources dictate their movements, and often travel many kilometres from a roost to a feeding site. A number of the parakeets remain on the eastern side and feed largely on *E. obliqua* and *E. viminalis* which bloom between February and April.

Although they mainly use Blue Gum and Black Gum as a nectar source during the breeding season, Swift Parakeets are known to feed on of 10 different eucalypts, out of the 29 recorded in Tasmania.

Reports of Musk Lorikeets and Swift Parakeets damaging ripening fruit in orchards are recorded. It appears that the parakeets mostly attack soft fruits such as apricots, peaches and plums (Brown 1989).

In flight, the Musk Lorikeet shows the diagnostic greenish under wing-coverts and yellow stripe on the side of the breast. © *Cyril Laubscher*

When feeding in fruit trees at a distance, a Musk Lorikeet resembles a Swift Parakeet, both being green overall. When flying, there is a distinct visual difference – the Musk Lorikeet has green under wing-coverts, compared to the red of the Swift Parakeet.

PUBLICITY AND EDUCATION AID RECOVERY PLAN

The scientific work that is being done under the Swift Parrot Recovery Plan is of great importance, and is being brought to public attention.

Two pages of Swift Parrot news, prepared by Anna Knee and Raymond Brereton (PWS Tasmania) were published in issue 6 (September 1998) of the "Volunteer", the newsletter of the Threatened Bird Network.

"Swifts Across The Strait" is a 12 page newsletter that was prepared by Wendy Vella and Simon Kennedy in

Victoria. This was distributed to volunteers involved in the mainland winter counts to provide them with feedback from their efforts.

Schools have been targeted, and the Swift Parrot Rehabilitation Network is a program that is currently operating in 14 rural and urban schools in eastern Tasmania. The rehabilitation of Swift Parakeet habitat is the main objective of the program, as its name implies. The planting of Blue Gum and Black Gum on sites within the local area of participating schools is being undertaken. Eight sites have already been planted, with other sites being sought for future rehabilitation.

Bev Sharman, the proprietor of Forest Glen Tea Gardens at Spreyton in northern Tasmania, undoubtedly has the birds' interest in mind. For many years, she has been feeding, and publicising, the plight of the Swift Parakeet to visitors at the tea gardens.

This generous lady, because of her deep concern for the declining population of Swift Parakeets, has now purchased and obtained around 52,000 Blue Gum seedlings for distribution to, and planting by, farmers in her vicinity. The planting of such large numbers is impressive, and this can only benefit the wild population of Swift Parakeets in time to come. However, it will probably take around 100 years for the seedlings to have grown large enough to supply the much-needed nesting sites that will aid the breeding situation.

At the tea gardens, she feeds many Swift Parakeets that fly in each day to feed on her home-made mixture

of water, mixed with raw sugar and bread, to provide a porridge consistency that is eaten by the parakeets. However, the Tasmania Parks and Wildlife Service and Brett Gartrell are carefully monitoring this mixture – to assist Bev Sharman in ensuring that it does not have an adverse long-term effect on the wild population.

This unique red Swift Parakeet was seen in a flock feeding at the Forest Glen Tea Gardens at Spreyton, Tasmania. © *Bev Sharman*

CENTRESPREAD (OVERLEAF): A rapidly-flying Swift Parakeet can attain, and possibly sustain, a speed of between 70-80 km (45-50 mph) when migrating across the Bass Strait from Tasmania to Victoria. © *Cyril Laubscher*

THE SWIFT PARAKEET IN AVICULTURE

The Swift Parakeet is an enigmatic species that has puzzled scientists and taxonomists since it was first discovered. Taxonomically, they are not sure whether it is a parakeet or a lorikeet, as it has affinities with a number of parakeets, yet has many of the habits of a lorikeet, which probably developed as a result of convergent evolution.

A similar situation prevails in aviculture in that some breeders treat it as a parakeet, and others as a combination of both parakeet and lorikeet. One breeder, in response to a questionnaire, stated definitely that it is not a lorikeet and should never be given nectar.

This Australian-bred Swift Parakeet shows greater luminosity and brighter colouring than European-bred birds. © Cyril Laubscher

In fact, during the breeding season in the wild, the Swift Parakeet lives entirely on nectar, pollen, insects and lerp. No seed has been found in any of the gut contents of birds taken for post mortem examination during the breeding season in Tasmania. Yet, every breeder surveyed globally, has offered either hard, or soaked seed to the breeding pairs during the breeding season. Why is this done? Probably because, in most cases, it is thought that this is the correct diet. And, as a certain amount of breeding success is achieved, there is no need to do anything different. In many instances, the seed diet is supplemented with a whole range of other foods that constitute a better, and hopefully, a more balanced diet. This will be dealt with at greater length in *The Importance of Nutrition* section.

There is no doubt that breeders have made great inroads in establishing the Swift Parakeet in aviculture. Considering that there has been no legal exportation of Swift Parakeets from Australia – except to zoos – in the last 40-50 years, this is a great achievement for aviculture.

AVICULTURAL STATUS

It is estimated that there are around 7,000 Swift Parakeets kept in Holland, Belgium, Denmark and Germany. Breeders in these four countries have achieved the greatest success. France is another country where increased breeding results have been reported during the last three years. There are also a good number of breeders in other European countries.

Globally, I would expect that the worldwide avicultural population should exceed 10,000+. This would be much greater than the estimated wild population in Australia. Aviculturists can, and should, continue the important role that they have done until now, in preserving this species for future generations.

In some countries, there appears to be a decline in numbers bred. In Germany, this is particularly noticeable. Renate Erlenbröker, the chairperson of the parrot breeders society AZ AGZ, sent in the following figures that were received from breeders of Swift Parakeets for 1996 – 308 young bred from 104 pairs. In 1997, only 242 were reared from 76 pairs. The average number of 3 young from each pair is a good figure by international standards, and is in line with other statistics received from various countries.

In Denmark, Morten Bruun-Rasmussen states that Swift Parakeets are now plentiful.

Australian breeders have difficulty in obtaining them on the mainland, and they are one of the rarest parakeets in Australian aviaries. Breeders in Tasmania are not allowed to sell Swift Parakeets. They also have to obtain a licence to keep any. It is estimated that there are less than 100 left in Australian aviaries.

In South Africa, a similar number are kept. Gavin Zietsman from the Johannesburg area is now accumulating a viable number of breeding pairs from different gene pools, to ensure that this beautiful species survives in South African aviculture.

In the USA and Canada, they are rare in aviculture. This could be because so many parrots are bred mainly for the pet market, and this species is not perceived to be a justifiable candidate for pet status.

HOUSING AND GENERAL MANAGEMENT

Most breeders house Swift Parakeets in outdoor aviaries. Others use a combination of an outdoor aviary with an unheated indoor flight attached. Only a few keep them in heated indoor flights, while more keep them in unheated indoor flights. Where the degree of cold climate is excessive in winter, breeders house them in combined outside aviaries with heated indoor flights. Some of the more experienced breeders have used multiple housing methods over a period of time.

Aviaries in warm climates

In Australia, South Africa, and California, the warm to hot climatic conditions eliminate the need for a birdroom or indoor shelter, even in winter. However, aviary designs there usually incorporate a sheltered section, where the birds can roost, feed, and breed.

In hot climates, there must be some sort of shading and shelter provided. A free flow of air circulation should be allowed, wherever possible. Shade cloth raised and supported, above the wire roof of an aviary, is useful. Another benefit of shade cloth is in preventing the Swift Parakeets from taking immediate fright at the sight of a hawk or falcon above the aviary – the results of which can be quite devastating.

Tom Mossop, an Australian breeder who lives in Victoria, recalls an unfortunate incident that happened in his aviary in 1994. Five young Swift Parakeets that had been reared in one nest were suddenly startled when a sparrowhawk landed on an adjoining aviary. Within one hour, 4 young had died – with two still clinging to the perch after they had died. The fifth youngster is still suffering from stress-induced acute feather loss, and is unlikely ever to recover. One of the 4 young that died was sent to the Department of Veterinary Studies at Melbourne University, where a rigorous post mortem study could not establish any cause of death.

Dudley Williams from Edmonton in Queensland, also lost 5 young in one morning from a Brown Goshawk attack. Breeding adults then stopped breeding because of the Brown Goshawk presence. Rob McGuinness in Tasmania had a similar problem with a Goshawk. No other breeder outside of Australia has reported any difficulties with birds of prey.

Single breeding flights are generally 0.9-1m (3+ ft) wide x 1.8-2.4m (6-8 ft high), and anywhere from 1.8m up to 6m (6-20 ft) or more, in length. Southern hemisphere breeders often construct their aviaries out of metal. In the accompanying photograph, a detached aviary with covered roof and sides on the shelter, houses a single breeding pair of Swift Parakeets in Tasmania.

Colony aviaries can be much larger, depending on the available space and the number of birds it is intended to house. There is no doubt that the larger the aviary, the better it is for the Swift Parakeets in terms of flying and exercising space, another

A single detached aviary, with a sheltered section, houses a breeding pair of Swift Parakeets in Tasmania. © Cyril Laubscher

important factor that helps to overcome any obesity problems. Obesity all too frequently arises when the aviary space is too small, and this condition is aggravated when the birds are fed on an overly rich diet throughout the year.

Because they are a gregarious species, Swift Parakeets can safely be housed as a colony, or as a group with doves, finches, softbills, and other small, docile parakeets like Splendid and Turquoisine Parakeets.

Smaller outdoor, sheltered aviaries can be made to look extremely attractive, with growing plants and flowers softening the overall appearance. The boards covering the bottom half of this aviary, which is only open on two sides at the top, provides further protection for small ground-dwelling species like quail. An unheated shelter at the back offers adequate protection on cold wintry nights. The roof can be covered in clear or frosted corrugated plastic or perspex sheeting for protection from wild bird droppings.

A planted aviary is an ideal place to house them, as they are not normally destructive to plants, apart from perhaps nibbling away at flowers that contain some pollen or nectar. In fact, plants that produce a good amount of pollen will certainly

An attractive aviary for Swift Parakeets, with growing plants and flowers softening the overall appearance. © *Colin Lawrence*

aid the breeding results, as the intake of pollen and insects during the breeding season in the wild, provides the necessary protein for the young nestlings. They will also search for, and consume, insects.

Newly fledged young through to the age of six months are very susceptible to stress. To avoid any serious injuries or fatalities, a natural barrier of climbing or other plants growing at the opposite end of a lengthy flight will prevent them from breaking their necks if suddenly frightened.

European and North American housing

Breeders of Swift Parakeets in the northern hemisphere have a choice of using an outdoor aviary combined with a heated or unheated indoor flight, or a purpose-built birdroom with heated or unheated indoor flights. Prevailing winter conditions will generally determine whether heated quarters are necessary, or not. A frost-free environment is ideal for them and unheated premises do not present any difficulties for this active little parakeet.

It is not necessary to heat the inside of the birdroom excessively – maintaining the temperature at 10°C is more than adequate in winter.

When planning to convert a large establishment into a birdroom, a number of indoor flights 0.9m (3 feet) wide x 1.8-2.4m (6-8 feet) high and 3m (10 feet), or longer, can be built. A 0.9m (3 feet) wide passage running the length of the building allows easy access for feeding the birds, and doubles up as a safety porch when a door is closed at the end. This prevents the birds from escaping should one get out of its aviary.

A former warehouse has been completely refurbished as a birdroom by the well-known Dutch breeder, Kees Lansen – seen here feeding his birds. This change has provided excellent accommodation for his Swift Parakeets. Feeding hatches were placed in front to make feeding easier.

Adequate ventilation must be provided during the hot spells that can occur in summer. The heat must not become excessive for

Swift Parakeets, especially when young have started growing their feathers. At this stage, they are vulnerable to overheating when the temperature climbs over 30-35°C.

In discussion with various breeders worldwide, it is probably a good idea to start cooling down the aviary or birdroom as soon as the temperature reaches 30°C. A number of breeders have lost complete nests of young through heat exhaustion when the temperature climbed to the high thirties!

A fully equipped kitchen with a refrigerator, and worktops with kitchen sink and running water is almost an essential in a larger breeding establishment. Food preparation and the washing of dishes – preferably stainless steel, plastic, or porcelain – is another important consideration in the modern day birdroom. A dishwasher is a useful and hygienic accessory. If running water can be piped to automatically fill water bowls, then it will lessen the workload considerably. A further use for running water is to operate an automatic mist spray for cooling down the premises during excessively hot spells, and the birds can bathe in the misty rain. Mist spraying can reduce the temperature by 2-3°C in hot weather.

Swift Parakeets love to bathe, and as soon as their water bowl is replenished, they are likely to head straight down to it. Because of their liquid droppings, it is essential for them to have fresh water daily for bathing.

Another useful accessory is a video camera on an overhead tracking system. Operated by remote control from the comfort of the home, it can be controlled to monitor movements and activities of the birds in their aviaries, especially during the breeding season.

The benefit of a birdroom is that the birds are not subjected to the harsh elements, but it also deprives them of bathing naturally during a rainfall. Rain can assist in keeping their plumage in good condition. Natural sunlight is normally denied to birds in a birdroom, unless there are plenty of windows, which then create a problem during hot, sunny spells. Some form of blind is necessary if all the windows cannot be opened to allow fresh air to circulate and cool down the interior.

Where there is a marked variance between summer and winter – removable glass or plastic panels can be fixed to outdoor aviaries to prevent the prevailing cold winds in some areas from blowing right across the outdoor aviaries.

The number of different aviary designs, sizes and styles varies greatly around the world. The most important consideration in each climatic region is the welfare of the birds. If they are well catered for, their breeding potential improves.

Another alternative design which can be used for Swift Parakeets is shown here where a birdroom is made to look much more attractive, yet functional, through the careful use of space, plants, and light. The overall appearance is aesthetically pleasing, and the breeding results achieved by this breeder have proved that the forethought and planning in this neatly laid out birdroom – with outdoor aviaries attached – has paid dividends.

This attractive wooden-built aviary, with plants, is ideal accommodation for Swift Parakeets.
© Cyril Laubscher

THE IMPORTANCE OF NUTRITION

Because their lifestyle in the wild has not been fully understood in the past, aviculturists have not had much information on which to base the nutritional requirements of the Swift Parakeet in their aviaries, and more so, when they breed. Most have followed what other breeders have done, and in some cases, have inherited the problems that are occasionally associated with individual birds from their previous owners, especially if the birds are older specimens.

Food consumption in the wild during the breeding season

Brett Gartrell's PhD study involves investigating the physiological and nutritional constraints on the Swift Parakeet reproduction cycle. This includes various aspects of biological behaviour, and nutrition requirements. He has already found that during the breeding season in the wild, the Swift Parakeet lives entirely on nectar, pollen, insects and lerp. No seed has been found in any of the gut contents of birds taken by him for post mortem examination during the breeding season in Tasmania.

Other feeding trials are being conducted on the captive population of 17 Swift Parakeets held at the University of Tasmania research aviaries in Hobart. One of the trials in particular that could have a major influence on Swift Parakeet feeding involves the use of pellets with nectar and water only.

Gartrell chose to use pelleted diets for a number of reasons, the main one being that he could not afford to have vitamin and mineral deficiencies interfering with the research trial. He mentioned that it is well established that putting the birds onto a diet of nectar, seed, and fruit only, is going to leave them deficient in Vitamin A, D, E, and possibly Calcium and Potassium. He needed uniform food quality throughout the trial, and

Lerp under the leaves is an important part of a Swift Parakeet's natural diet. Note the damage to the leaves from the insects that secrete the sugary-coated lerp. © Chris Tzaros

pelleted diets are far less likely to have aflatoxins and varying levels of nutrients throughout various seasons.

The three stainless steel pots contain nectar, water, and pellets used in the research aviaries. © Cyril Laubscher

One of the changes that could take place is that the musculature of the Swift Parakeets' gizzard could possibly change with the use of a soft food or hard food diet. When 5 of the birds that had been on the pelleted ration were dissected, the gizzard showed no change to that of a bird that had been on a seed and vegetable diet.

Gartrell placed 4 birds – 2 from the wild and 2 from a wildlife carer working for Tasmanian Parks and Wildlife Service – in one of the research aviaries as sole occupants two years ago. During the ensuing period, they have been fed only on pellets, water, and nectar. When the carer's specimens were obtained, they had been fed on a seed and nectar ration for 12 months and were in poor feather condition with many stress bars showing in the feathers. After 2 years on the pellet, nectar and water ration, they are in immaculate feather condition. The photograph of these 4 birds was taken in July 1999, when they had been on the special ration for 21 months.

This group of Swift Parakeets, in superb feather condition, have been fed on pellets, nectar, and water only, for the last two years at the University of Tasmania research aviaries in Hobart. © Cyril Laubscher

The final results could possibly take another three years before being completed and published. Swift Parakeet breeders will undoubtedly benefit in having a better understanding of the nutritional requirements of this specialised parakeet, especially the constitution of the nectar, which commercial producers can then try to formulate and match.

Foods that are mainly used by breeders

Replies to the questionnaires revealed that seed, nectar, softfood, wild grass seed and weeds, greenfood, sprouted seed, fruit, and to a lesser extent vegetables, along with some insects including mealworms, are being fed regularly by breeders worldwide. Grit and sand must always be available.

Swift Parakeets should have as varied a diet as possible, to ensure that a balanced diet is consumed. Individual birds will have preferences for certain foods at particular times of the year. Check with the breeder when the birds are purchased as to which foods have been fed in the past, and follow that while gradually introducing changes – if necessary – to improve their breeding potential. All of the following foods can be used. In the winter rest period after the moult, the amount of fattening foods should be reduced to offset the possibility of obesity.

Nectar

Nectar, either commercial or homemade, is offered by more than 60% of breeders, most of whom opt to use a brand of commercial nectar that is easily prepared. Check the ingredients of commercial nectar carefully to ensure that the Swift Parakeets are not being fed on overly fat nectar, especially if the birds are housed in a smaller aviary. Commercial nectars contain much of the nutrients, amino-acids and protein necessary for the birds welfare. All nectar must be fed fresh daily, and in warmer climates, twice daily.

> Gartrell states (in litt.) "My overall impression is that the Swift Parakeet is primarily a nectarivorous and insectivorous bird. The enlarged gizzard allows it to use seed in captivity, but this is not its "natural" diet. While nectar plays an important role in energy supply especially during the breeding season, pollen and insects are needed to fulfil its protein requirements"

Some homemade recipes are tried and tested over many years, but avoid using any unnecessary fatty or oily ingredients. Some breeders do not supply nectar at all, and yet, this is the mainstay of their diet in the wild.

Pollen

Pollen is an important source of food during the breeding season in Tasmania, as along with insects, it supplies much of the Swift Parakeet's protein needs.

Feeding commercial bee pollen is beneficial, even if only about 7-10% of it is actually digested. It can be fed as it is, mixed into nectar, or in a soft food mixture. Some breeders are already using pollen.

Cut garden flowers and weeds – especially those laden with pollen where bees are seen feeding – and hang them up in the aviary so that the birds can nibble at the flowers. In the same way, unsprayed apple or other fruit tree twigs laden with blossom appeals to Swift Parakeets, and provides fresh bark that they can chew.

Swift Parakeets are continually on the move or flying about. An interesting sight is to see how playful and acrobatic they are when feeding on a branch of blossom hung vertically from a hook in the roof of their aviary.

Blossoms offer small amounts of pollen, an essential ingredient in the diet of a Swift Parakeet. © Cyril Laubscher

Softfood

In the survey softfood was used by 67 (93%) of the breeders, with commercial brands leading by nearly 2 to 1 against homemade soft food. This was supplied fresh every day during the breeding season.

Nearly 60% of the breeders continued supplying softfood between 2-3 times per week during the year, with some feeding it daily. Small quantities are advisable.

A variety of softfoods is available commercially, most of which are egg and biscuit based. In the breeding season, rearing food should be offered daily when young are in the nest. Swift Parakeets will come down to this first as soon as it is

This freshly prepared softfood for Swift Parakeets contains sprouted seed mixed with 13 other ingredients. It must be refrigerated and used within 3 days. © Cyril Laubscher

placed on the feeding tray. Two or three different mixtures can be used at different times of the year, depending on whether it is the resting period or the breeding season.

Is seed important for Swift Parakeets?

In the wild, Swift Parakeets consume some seed, but not during the breeding season. Seed, especially *Eucalyptus* spp. was found in the stomach contents of Swift Parakeets taken on the Australian mainland in winter. Small caterpillars and other vegetable matter, sand and grit were found in stomachs (Hindwood and Sharland 1964).

Every breeder who responded to the questionnaire feeds seed in one form or another. Most of them feed dry seed throughout the year, others supply sprouted seed only when young are in the nest. However, dry seed should only be a supplementary food to nectar, soft food, fruit and vegetables.

Mixed small parakeet seed, followed closely by sunflower and then safflower – both of which are normally included in the more popular seed mixtures – are the seeds most breeders use.

A small parakeet mixture is widely used, and is readily available from seed merchants. A good seed mixture for a daily diet should concentrate on various millets, canary, and oats, and have the minimum amount of fatty or oily seeds – like sunflower, rape, niger, hemp, poppy and sesame. This will assist in combating obesity, which is a major problem.

The following mixtures are some of the daily food rations prepared for Swift Parakeets by Kees Lansen.

Commercial parrot food mixture
Commercial lory food
Apple
Rose Hips cut up
Juniper berries
Commercial insectivorous mixture

Commercial softfood mixture
Dandelion cut up in small pieces
Commercial egg-based rearing food
Sprouted seed
Pear
Commercial pollen
Fine minerals (used for racing pigeons)

© Cyril Laubscher

Sprouted seeds

Sprouted seeds are a highly nutritious food source. Many of the vitamins, minerals, and trace elements found in freshly sprouted seed. Sprouted small millets, canary, niger, buckwheat, safflower, mung beans and sunflower can all be mixed, and fed fresh daily when young are in the nest.

However, during the rest period, it is more beneficial to use various millets. This can be fed daily or 2-3 times per week. About a month or two prior to the breeding season, sunflower and the other fatty seed can be added in small quantities, about 10-12 sunflower seeds per pair. Increase this gradually as the breeding season approaches. Some breeders mix sprouted seeds in with the soft food mixture.

Chickweed is an excellent greenfood to feed to Swift Parakeets.
© Cyril Laubscher

Greenfood and vegetables

Greenfood, such as chickweed, dandeli and groundsel, plus any wild grass seed can be offered *ad lib* as they are very nutritious. Ensure that the greenfood is contaminated with chemicals. Avoid collecting greenfood along public footpaths, parks and public places whe council and municipalities control wee by using herbicides.

If seeding grass is home grown, then the should not be any contamination. The seeding heads of various millets, canary seed, and oats are extremely palatable t Swift Parakeets. They are readily grown warmer climates, and should preferably fed in the milky stage, before the heads ripen and dry out.

Carrot - grated, diced, or in strips - is favoured by mar breeders. Spinach is a useful leaf vegetable as is lettuce Some birds relish fresh corn on the cob. If frozen corn the cob is used, it needs to be thoroughly thawed out before feeding to the birds. Other vegetables used by o or two breeders are: cucumber, chicory, celery and beetroot.

Groundsel and Dandelion are avidly eaten by Swift Parakeets. © Cyril Laubscher

Fruit

Apples, especially the sweet Golden Delicious are the favourite with almost every breeder. Sweet oranges are second, followed by grape and pear. Other fruits used banana, kiwi, pomegranates (in season), plums, sweet mandarins, peaches, figs, melon (in Australia) strawberr raspberries, and cherries (in France). Rowanberries are sought, and some breeders use rose hips.

Insects

Surprisingly, not many breeders (only 11%) offer insects insectivorous food, yet in the wild, they are fed when yo are in the nest. An insectivorous food would supplement soft food, and provide extra protein and nourishment fo growing nestlings. Mealworms are held in the foot while soft inside is eaten. More breeders are using mealworms albeit sparingly (1-2 per bird per day) out of the breeding season. When young have hatched, increase the mealworm ration to about 4 for each young nestling, and more as they grow. Frozen ants eggs are availab and can be mixed in - when thawed - into the sprouted seed.

upplying willow and other non-toxic fresh cut fruit branches for nibbling – and as perches – they can
ny hidden minute insects while nibbling the bark.

t Parakeets must be fed fresh food daily. Kees Lansen is seen in the picture feeding his birds early in
morning. A trolley takes the hardship out of this chore. Clean stainless steel dishes and china bowls
illed, and placed on the feeding tray, which is accessed from the passageway in his large birdroom.

pellets replace seed eventually?

us breeders feed pellets to their Swift Parakeets these days. The tests being conducted by Gartrell
already borne interesting results, but it will take a while yet before the full data is forthcoming.

n Wilkinson, Curator of Lory Love near Johannesburg airport, South Africa, finds that it is difficult to wean
Parakeets onto alternative diets or foods, a sentiment that other breeders agree with. It takes much
nce and perseverance to change them onto new foods. There is also a natural aversion on the part of
lers to incorporate new ideas and implement change, even though they may be extremely beneficial.

eeders can overcome this aversion, pellets may be extremely useful. Because of the clean manufacturing
ess, pellets have many advantages over fresh food and dry seed, which can become contaminated in
aration. Wilkinson believes that a gradual introduction of pellets into the everyday avicultural diet for
pecies could be the best way forward.

sity is a problem

ity is becoming a greater factor in aviculture generally. When the breeding cycle alters, and productivity
down, especially with pairs that have produced good clutches and reared their young successfully in
ast, then this ailment should be one of the first to be considered, and possibly investigated.

In a similar way to the huma race, Swift Parakeets become obese through over indulgin the incorrect food. This is particularly so, because of th lack of knowledge of what i required to keep them on th correct diet.

Overweight or obese birds h difficulty in breeding, as thei fertility and egg laying will b affected, and the obesity cou eventually lead to heart dise

Regulating obesity is a slow process, and will take a considerable time. Avoid usi excessively fatty and oily foc ingredients and seeds, such

Sunflower seeds are very fattening and should be used sparingly.
© Cyril Laubscher

sunflower, hemp, rape, niger, poppy and sesame until the birds have returned to normal. Plenty of flyir exercise in a long flight will assist.

After Swift Parakeets have come through the annual moult, it is a good idea to alter some of the high fat content rations, or quantities thereof, so that they have a rest period from the rich food intake.

Instead, a low protein, high calcium diet with vitamin and mineral supplements can be offered durin the non-breeding period. Then, start to build them up for parental duties about two months before t breeding season approaches.

ACHIEVING BREEDING SUCCESS

When comparing the breeding information received from the questionnaires, the results during the la three breeding seasons show a fairly consistent breeding pattern. But, there is considerable variation between some countries and continents. And, many breeders complain about the loss of young nestlin which can be problematical to rear.

Two main factors have to be considered when breeding with Swift Parakeets. The first is the climate, a the second is the food. Both have a profound effect on the breeding activity and the survival of the resulting young. Excessive heat is a killer as is the incorrect food.

When young are in the nest, it is advisable to feed as great a variety of different foods, including softfo rearing food, nectar, greenfood, fruit and insects. The softfood can be quite viscous when adults are feeding young.

Sexing Swift Parakeets

Certain aviculturists have difficulty in ascertaining whether they have a genuine pair. If the birds are l than 12 months old, then this can be a problem – although, some long-term breeders have an ability t select an occasional true pair from good young. However, this sexing can occasionally be hit and miss especially when it is good female, and a not particularly colourful male.

Kees Lansen uses the following method to sex his birds. Check the under wing-coverts of a fledgling weaned young bird. Between the 5th and 12th primary feathers, there are little white spots that appe make a line of white dots (see colourful young male on front cover or in centrespread). When the feathers are blown upward, a second row of smaller white dots is revealed. This is constant on all you birds until they reach the age of 10-12 months when they start to go through a full moult.

Normally, males then lose the white spots and have a darker green back and mantle. Occasionally, som males will retain the white spots until the second moult. Females usually retain the white spots in

...hood. In adult females, the tips of the under tail-
...erts are green with a little yellow above. Adult males
...ay only a little yellow or red, but no green tips.

...atures and sexual maturity

...ng have a juvenile moult at 4-5 months and a full
...lt between 10-12 months. If young were bred in the
...round of a new season, they may be sufficiently
...ure to breed at 14-15 months. However, it is often
...er to wait until they reach full sexual maturity after
...second full moult, before trying to breed with them.

...s Lansen has one female that he bred in June 1997,
...ch then laid a round of 3 eggs in February 1998 –
...n she was only eight months old. Two of the eggs
...e fertile, but dead-in-shell. This is highly unusual to
...e a female lay at such a young age, and he would
...cate waiting until the birds were fully adult and able
...ope with the stress of raising good young. Only 50%
...oung would possibly be able to breed at 12-14
...ths.

...ny or single breeding pairs?

...use they are gregarious by nature, Swift Parakeets
...be bred on a colony system. Some breeders do
...emely well with colony breeding, but the general
...ensus is that when establishing a colony, the
...wing procedure must be followed.

...up the aviary first. If
...irs, or more are
...emplated, then
...tion 3 nestboxes of
...same size around the
...ry, all at the same
...ht (+ - 30cm) from
...oof of the aviary.
...preparing the
...ry, release all the
...s into the aviary
...ther. Some breeders
...cate using an extra
...le in a colony. When
...ony is established,
...ot place any new
...Parakeets in the aviary.

This young male illustrates the ideal colour, without
any flecking of red, on the breast. © Cyril Laubscher

Young and adult Swift Parakeets are housed together as a colony in this aviary.
© Colin Lawrence

...s procedure is not
...wed, and birds are added intermittently, then the following experience that one breeder in the UK
...is likely to occur. He bought 2 pairs and placed them in a combined indoor/outdoor aviary in 1996.
...2 pairs both bred and 4 young were reared. In 1997, another 2 new pairs were added, making a total
...pairs. The 2 pairs that bred in 1996 again laid and reared 8 young. In 1998, the original 2 pairs bred
...n with 9 young appearing on the perches. In 1999, the same 2 original pairs were double brooded,
...16 young were raised!

...the 2 pairs that were added in 1997 have not shown any sign of nesting, and this could be because
...original 2 pairs are dominant over the new introduced pairs.

Typical parakeet nestbox*

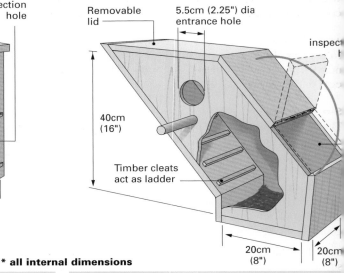

5.5cm (2.25") dia entrance hole

inspection hole

Removable lid

30-40cm (12-16")

Timber cleats act as ladder

20cm (8")

20cm (8")

Dutch nestbox*

Removable lid

5.5cm (2.25") dia entrance hole

inspect h

40cm (16")

Timber cleats act as ladder

20cm (8")

20cm (8")

* all internal dimensions

STANDARD NESTBOX

This nestbox is used worldwide by the majority of breeders. It can be obtained commercially, and is easily replaceable – from a hygienic point of view – at the end of the breeding season. Fill with suitable nesting material to 1-2 inches (25-50mm).

DUTCH NESTBOX

A nestbox that is popular with Dutch and continental breeders, who generally prefer to build the box from 1 inch (25mm) untreated soft pine board. This allows hygienic cleaning, and lasts much longer than any of the commercial glued boards.

Australian Pyramid nestbox*

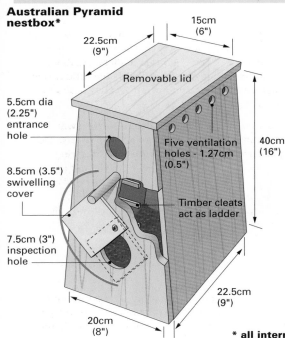

15cm (6")

22.5cm (9")

Removable lid

5.5cm dia (2.25") entrance hole

Five ventilation holes - 1.27cm (0.5")

40cm (16")

8.5cm (3.5") swivelling cover

Timber cleats act as ladder

7.5cm (3") inspection hole

22.5cm (9")

20cm (8")

Danish nestbox*

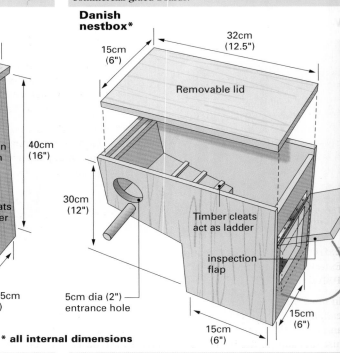

15cm (6")

32cm (12.5")

Removable lid

30cm (12")

Timber cleats act as ladder

inspection flap

5cm dia (2") entrance hole

15cm (6")

15cm (6")

* all internal dimensions

AUSTRALIAN PYRAMID NESTBOX

A nestbox design that is used by breeders in warmer climates, as the lid is removable to allow the nest to cool. By making a removable base for Swift Parakeets, the wet nesting material can be changed every 5 days, or change the box for a replica.

DANISH NESTBOX

Used by some breeders as an alternative to a standard nestbox as it allows the male to sleep or sit inside the top section, while the female incubates. The wooden cleats inside, can be nibbled into small pieces for lining. Nestboxes must be securely fixed.

Colony breeding has been practiced by most of the advanced breeders with many years of experience, without a great deal of success apparently. It could well be that they added new birds into an existing colony, upsetting the balance, and losing out on future breeding due to squabbling.

A select number of breeders are working with one male to two females in a small colony. Again the same rules apply about setting up. Two nestboxes are needed at the same height. Do not try to add another nestbox, as it is likely to cause desertion of the nestlings, should a female decide to lay a new clutch of eggs in the spare nestbox!

Single pairs to an aviary

There is a greater tendency to move towards a single pair to an aviary. This makes a lot of sense once a compatible pair is found. Those who have a fair number of young stock and spare birds can place them all together in one community flight. Then, let each male select the female of his choice – colour coded rings are essential for this operation – and separate out the chosen pair into their new breeding aviary or flight.

Two nestboxes can be placed in the aviary, and when the birds have chosen one it is advantageous to remove the second box just before, or shortly after the young have hatched. This is to eliminate the odd occasion when a female will start to lay another clutch while the chicks are still in the first nest, as they could die if not correctly fed.

Some breeders have found that leaving both nestboxes has induced the female to lay a second clutch, and she then leaves the final rearing of the young in the first nest to the male alone. This may work for some, but it is a gamble that is simply not worth it as both nests can be lost.

More control can be applied with a single pair. In a colony, there can be aggression, especially if one or two birds are not in full breeding condition. While this aggression seldom amounts to much, nevertheless, it is disruptive on occasions. This does not happen when they are housed as a single pair. Feeding is better controlled and allowance can be made depending on the number of young in the nest.

When to ring young nestlings

These young are almost ready to fledge.
© Kerry Febey

A female is likely to lay between 4-6 eggs, which hatch in 19-20 days. Young nestlings often hatch two days apart, and they must be close rung with a size L ring – 4,5 mm in diameter. Ringing must be done between 8-10 days of age. This is the official ring size as recommended by The Parrot Society in the UK. On the continent, a similar size is advocated.

In South Africa, Shaun Wilkinson (pers. comm.) rings swift nestlings with a 5 mm ring when they are around 12 days old. He has not experienced any problems with the larger ring. Nestlings fledge when they are around 35 days old and they only wean about 4-5 weeks later – a much longer period of weaning than parakeets normally need. Fledglings vary considerably in their colouring – some will carry more yellow, others may have red flecking.

Extreme heat can cause fatalities

Extreme heat affects Swift Parakeets greatly, especially when the nestlings are starting to feather from the 10th day onwards.

In Australia, depending on the heat and humidity levels, young nestlings can, and often do die from heat exhaustion, when temperatures climb above 30-35 degrees Celsius. Misting has to be introduced to try and lower the temperatures. Sometimes the young can survive a couple of warm days, but invariably, they must succumb to the heat, and the parents have no way of cooling them down.

Stan Sindel, well-known aviculturist and author from New South Wales, provided an important case study. In the 35 years that he has kept and bred Swift Parakeets, he has never managed to parent rear a single youngster – because they lay their eggs in November, and the young hatch in December. They only fledge in January when the weather is at its hottest, and the humidity is greatest. Instead, he has had to remove the young and hand-rear them as soon as they are 10 days old.

South Africa's climate is generally not quite as harsh as Australia's. Breeders have not experienced any great difficulties there.

Whenever outdoor or indoor temperatures start to climb over 28-30°C, it is advisable to implement so method of cooling the aviary. Opening the top of a nestbox may help.

Kees Lansen in Holland has experienced similar difficulties to Sindel. When the temperature in his ind birdrooms climbs above 35°C during the occasional hot spell, he has to use the overhead sprinkling system to cool down the birdrooms.

Over breeding can affect productivity

Some breeders seek three or more rounds of eggs per season. This, in the long term, can prove counte productive. When Swift Parakeets start to under perform, then it is time to consider, whether the bird obese, or have they been rearing too many clutches?

If each pair rears one good clutch, this is all that can be expected. If they rear a second round, then it should be considered a bonus. This is the maximum that a breeder can expect of any pair, even thoug some pairs will breed on if allowed to. It is better to have one or two full rounds of 3-5 young per co rather than only 1-2 young in each of three rounds. A rest period is necessary and it is up to the indiv breeder to consider what his objectives are. The welfare of the birds is uppermost in the mind of a go breeder, as well as the breeding results.

Record keeping

Kees Lansen has been breeding Swift Parakeets for 17 years now, and when I asked him what happen when he first began breeding, he was able to pull out a record card for each and every pair that he possessed since he started. He could tell me when the eggs were laid, how many were fertile, how m hatched, and the total that were successfully reared. Kees Lansen is not unique, but he is typical of a g breeder, many of whom would have similar records.

SWIFT PARAKEET MUTATIONS

Pastel mutation

In 1982, the first mutation was bred – the Pastel. All the colours are diluted in this autosomal recessive mutation.

The breeding expectation for the Pastel is: All Pastel young will be bred when paired to another Pa When paired to a normal, expect 1 Pastel in 4 young – the other three will be two Normal/Pastel a one normal.

Grey Green mutation

The Grey Green is a relatively new mutation. A female is portrayed. This primary mutation will breed Grey Green young when paired to a Normal, as the Grey Green is dominant over the Normal. The alternative name of Olive is used in the Benelux countries. A double factor has now apparently been and it is said to be slightly darker in colour than the single factor shown.

Red-bellied mutation

The Red-bellied is a colourful mutation, where the red can extend up to the breast. Young bred from mutation are normal looking with some red spots, and the full red belly colouring only appears after second full moult.

Pastel Blue mutation

In Denmark, Leif Jørgensen bred the first Pastel Blue mutation in 1994. The young were subsequently to a breeder in Odense. Morten Bruun-Rasmussen (pers. comm.) says that the colour was not very appealing, and there was not much interest shown by other breeders. Nothing has been heard about mutation since then, and it is feared that it may have died out.

this action picture, the diluted underwing colour of the Pastel utation can be seen. The extent of the yellowish underparts is mediately apparent, and the lighter flesh-coloured feet and enails of this mutation are clearly visible. © *Cyril Laubscher*

From the rear, the dilution of the mantle, back and wing colour
in the Pastel mutation is visible. The male is on the left.
© Cyril Laubscher

PASTEL MUTATION

The frontal view of the Pastel mutation reveals
how the overall colour is diluted.
© Cyril Laubscher

GREY GREEN MUTATION

As far as is known, this mutation was first bred in Belgium. One breeder in Holland paired a Grey Green male to a Normal female, and bred three young – all Grey Green. This breeding result substantiates that it is a dominant mutation, which, will produce Grey Green young when paired with a Normal, or a Pastel mutation. A double factor has now apparently been bred, that is said to be slightly darker in colour than the single factor shown.
© Cyril Laubscher

From the rear, overall differe between the G Green mutatio female and a Normal male very marked.
© Cyril Laubs

This study clearly shows the difference between a Grey Green mutation female, and a Normal male.
© Cyril Laubscher

RED-BELLIED MUTATION

A Red-bellied and a Pastel mutation are examples of the variety in mutations that will soon start to develop. There is a likelihood of a Red-bellied Pastel appearing eventually.
© Cyril Laubscher

The colourful Red-bellied is a much sought after colour variation. After the second full moult, a male can have red right up to the chest. Fledglings only show a few flecks of red, which gradually increase with each moult. The inheritance of this mutation is not yet fully understood, but it does appear to be a "progressive" mutation, in that the colour develops over a period of time. Any young bred from an adult Red-bellied mutation should be kept for at least two years to ensure that the colour is fully developed.
© Cyril Laubscher

The Red-bellied mutation male displays the striking colour of the under tail-coverts as it adopts an acrobatic pose. The other bird is a Pastel mutation male. © Cyril Laubscher

VETERINARY ASPECTS AND HEALTH CARE

© Text by Alan Jones B.Vet. Med, M.R.C.V.S.

Captive Swift Parakeets appear to suffer very little from disease problems, but obviously could be susceptible to accident or injury associated with a confining environment. Wire, zinc, plants, predators, other birds, or panic attacks are all possible causes of poisoning or injury to these birds.

Any bird which appears in a state of shock, or is subdued and fluffed-up, should be removed from the flight and placed in a warm environment – preferably a hospital cage or near a heat source – and offered electrolytes and glucose in water. Veterinary assistance should then be sought to pursue the diagnosis and correct treatment. It is worth finding the nearest veterinarian that has experience and expertise with birds, before a problem arises.

Worms need controlling

There are perhaps two major disease conditions to consider in this species. The first is INTERNAL PARASITISM – or infestation with worms. Like most of the small Australasian parakeets and Cockatiels, the Swift is particularly susceptible, with roundworms being more usual than tapeworms. The eggs are ingested from the ground via droppings passed from an infected bird, and the eggs rapidly develop through larval stages to adult worms in the gut of the parakeet.

Mildly infested birds will simply show as "poor doers", progressing to loss of weight in spite of a good appetite, dirty vent and diarrhoea, and poor feathering. Severe cases will be lethargic, and may die with intestines totally impacted with worms.

The answer is to dose all such birds on a regular basis with a suitable anthelminthic ("wormer"). This means any new bird on arrival; adult pairs before the breeding season and again after the young are raised; and the young birds after fledging and weaning. Most stock should be dosed routinely 3 - 4 times a year.

There are several suitable drugs on the market – specific names and dosages are not appropriate here since avian medicine advances at a rapid rate, and different preparations may be available in different countries. Ask your avian veterinarian for his/her advice. Control depends upon the removal of infective droppings from where the bird can reach them – by having suspended flights, or floors that are easily hosed down and washed.

Chlamydiosis and Psittacosis

The second important disease condition is CHLAMYDIOSIS. This is widespread among avian species worldwide, and is caused by an infectious bacteria-like organism called *Chlamydia psittaci*. It is more commonly known by the alternative name of PSITTACOSIS, which strictly speaking refers to the disease as found in psittacine birds.

It is estimated that 1% of wild birds are infected and act as carriers, and transmission is by inhalation of dust from infected droppings. In the wild state, with fit birds living in equilibrium with their environment the disease appears to cause little problem. Any stress factor (capture, travel, change or loss of food, moulting, etc) will increase shedding of the organism and will lower birds' resistance to infection.

There are several difficulties encountered in dealing with the disease. The first is the presence of carrier birds, which may themselves show no symptoms of disease. The second is the extremely variable incubation period from the time of infection to the development of clinical symptoms, which may vary from as little as 10 days to as long as 9 - 12 months. This fact makes identifying the source of infection very difficult. The third problem is the very variable signs shown by an infected bird – from none at all in the carrier state; through vague malaise; to depression, weight loss, green droppings and nasal discharge in the classic case; to sudden death with no warning signs.

The fourth point is the difficulty in specific diagnosis: there are currently several tests available, but none is 100% accurate. Space (and again the rapid advances in avian veterinary science, which render much written work out of date before it is published) precludes detailed discussion of the tests available, and the same applies to treatment. Suffice to say that involvement with an experienced avian veterinarian is required. The fifth problem is that prolonged treatment with an appropriate antibiotic is required to properly eliminate the infection. Short courses may suppress the infection so that the bird improves, but will not effect a complete cure.

The final point about the disease is its human significance: it can transfer to people and may cause a serious respiratory infection – similar to influenza, with headache, dry cough, tight chest, fever – but with possible serious consequences in the very young or elderly, or those with bronchitis or asthma. It can be treated easily in humans with the right antibiotic – *provided it is diagnosed early enough*.

If these two major diseases are avoided, and the birds are given good quality food and managed well, they should live long and healthy lives.

REFERENCES

Forshaw, J. M. **Australian Parrots** (second [revised] edition) Lansdowne Editions, Melbourne, Australia : 1981

Brown, P. B. **The Swift Parrot: A Report on its ecology, distribution and status, including management considerations** Department of Lands Parks and Wildlife, Tasmania: July 1989

Brereton, Raymond N. **Swift Parrot Recovery Plan 1997-1999** Nature Conservation Branch, Parks and Wildlife Service, 134 Macquarie Street, Hobart, Tas. 7000

Gartrell Brett D., Jones Susan M., Brereton Raymond N, Astheimer Lee B. **Morphological adaptations to nectarivory in the gastrointestinal tract of the swift parrot Lathamus discolor** School of Zoology, University of Tasmania, GPO Box 252-5, Hobart, Tas. 7001

Lindwood, K. A and Sharland, Michael **The Swift Parrot** The Emu, Vol. 64, March 1964, pp. 310-326

Kennedy, Simon and Vella, Wendy **Swifts Across The Strait** Flora and Fauna Branch, Natural Resource and Environment, PO Box 3100, Bendigo. Vic. 3554

Hutchins, B. R. & Lovell, R. H. **Australian Parrots: A field and Aviary Study** Avicultural Society of Australia, Melbourne, Australia: 1985

Christidis, L., Schodde, R., Shaw, D.D & Maynes, F.N. (1991). **Relationships among the Australo-Papuan Parrots, Lorikeets and Cockatoos** (Aves: Psittaciformes): Protein evidence Condor 93:302-317.

ACKNOWLEDGEMENTS

The Parrot Society UK, and Cyril Laubscher, would like to thank the following people for their assistance and information while preparing the editorial and photographic material for this book.

Our special thanks to:

Peter Brown, Raymond Brereton, Mark Holdsworh, and David James, of the Nature Conservation Branch, Department of Primary Industry, Water and Environment in Tasmania, Australia – for their assistance in the field, and in supplying the reports from which much of the editorial material and data relating to the Swift Parakeet in the wild, has been obtained.

Brett Gartrell, School of Zoology, University of Tasmania – for his invaluable assistance with all aspects of nutrition.

Chris Tzaros, Bev Sharman, and Kerry Febey, (Australia), Colin Lawrence (UK), Morten Bruun-Rasmussen (Denmark) – for providing photographic material.

Alan Jones (UK) – for his veterinary editorial contribution.

Simon Kennedy – for his editorial contribution.

Bertus & Mia Lansen (Holland), Kees Lansen (Holland), Stan and Jill Sindel (NSW, Australia), Don and Gwenda Coombe (Tasmania, Australia) Johnny and Thora Zietsman (Gauteng, South Africa) – for their kind hospitality while photographing for this book.

Jan van Mackelenbergh (Holland), Didier Leportois (France), and Richard Haldemann (Switzerland) – for their editorial input, translating, posting, and collating the replies to the questionnaires received from breeders.

Joseph Forshaw, Graeme Hyde, John Buchan, Tom De Graaff, and Ken Harwood (Australia) – for providing assistance with introductions to various contributors and breeders.

David and Vera Dennison/Avizandum (South Africa), Parkieten Sociëteit (Holland), and CDE/Club des Oiseaux Exotique (France) – for publishing advertisements.

Louis Bothma, Dave Russell (South Africa), Dick Schroeder (USA), Dave Longo (Canada), and Peter Them (Denmark) – for providing assistance with introductions to various contributors and breeders.

The 72 Swift Parakeet breeders from 11 countries, who have participated in supplying information for this book are:

Kurt Alessandri (Switzerland); John Appleton (UK); Johan Bakker (Holland); John Beardmore (Queensland, Australia); Adolf Bischofberger (Switzerland); Arnold Blaauwijkel (Holland); Tony Brindly (Victoria, Australia); Claude Brun (France); Morten Bruun-Rasmussen (Denmark); Bennie Bulter (Holland); Hermien Bunder (South Africa); Roland Chilvers (UK); Brett & Diane Cooke (Tasmania, Australia); Serge Courbaigts (France); Hans Creyghton (Holland); Wim de Groot (Holland); Kees de Leeuw (Holland); Francis Desbiaux (France); Eric Detienne (France); Michel Dotta (France); Alex & Lyn Dubois (UK); Dan Fanetti (WA Australia); Louis Faure (France); Kerry Febey (Tasmania, Australia); Mike Flikkema (Canada); Marco Fox (Holland); Emil Frey (Switzerland); Franz Fuglister (South Africa); Sonja Gautschi (Switzerland); Ken Harwood (WA Australia); Bennie Heller (Holland); John Hofer (Switzerland); Max Hunziker (Switzerland); Theo Imfeld Switzerland); Jan Jansen (Holland); Steen Bang Jensen (Greenland); Walter Kehl (Switzerland); Yannick Kerdoncuff (France); A Knoppert (Holland); Paul Lacournet (France); Kees Lansen (Holland); Gerard Larrouy (France); Colin Lawrence (UK); Jörg Lüscher (Switzerland); Rob McGuinness (Tasmania, Australia); Marcel Mertens (Belgium); Siggie Meyer (USA); Tom Mossop (Victoria, Australia); Daniel Mourgous (France); Karl-Heinz Müller (Germany); Jörg & Renate Erlenbröker (Germany); Terry Norman (UK); Serge Nussbaumer Switzerland); Anton Rijkers (Holland); Derek Ruff (UK); Werner Sahli (Switzerland); Edwin Schoones (Holland); Stan Sindel (NSW Australia); Mick Southey (UK); Harry Stephan (South Africa); Jan Stevens (Holland); Hans Stirnimann (Switzerland); John Talbot (UK); John van den Burgt (Holland); Mieke van der Tas (South Africa); Anton van der Wulp (Holland); J. Visscher (Holland); Albert Wellenzohn (Switzerland); Rolf & Sonia Wenger (Switzerland); Shaun Wilkinson (South Africa); Dudley Williams (Queensland, Australia); Ben Workel (Holland); Nick Yeo (UK); Gavin Zietsman; Johnny & Thora Zietsman (South Africa); Aris Zomer (Holland).